WHY *Sally* CAN'T PREACH

JACOB TANNER

Why Sally Can't Preach

Published by G3 Press
4979 GA-5
Douglasville, GA 30135
www.G3Min.org

Printed in the United States of America by Graphic Response, Atlanta, GA.

ISBN: 978-1-959908-08-1

Cover Design: Scott Schaller

Contents

Introduction

Gender roles govern the sexes.

That may seem like a strange claim in the postmodernity of the twenty-first century, but it's true and inescapable. It has also been fundamentally understood for the better part of human history. Study the major cultures and kingdoms of world history, and you will find irrefutable evidence that men have predominantly led society. Whether it was men leading the family, the state, or the church, society has long been imbued with patriarchal tendencies because that's the way God has designed the world. Men are to lead, especially within the church.

The very fact that men and women have been created *differently* by God should give us pause and contemplation. Men have been created by God and equipped to perform very specific functions, while women have also been created by God and equipped to perform very specific functions. While there is some overlap between the sexes (both, after all, are capable of walking, eating, talking, etc.), the physiology of men and women makes it abundantly clear that the teleology of the sexes is imbued within the Creator's design for them. Women are equipped to bear, nurture, and raise children. Weaker than men, they are nonetheless equipped to help man in the mission that the Lord has entrusted him with. Man, as the stronger sex, is equipped to conquer and take dominion of the world through the spread of the gospel, provide for his family, and defend his wife and children. Things have turned on their heads when men think they can bear children and women believe they are stronger than men.

When it comes to healthy churches, and even orthodox churches, it is essential that strong and biblically qualified *men* fill the pulpits and shepherd the flocks entrusted to their care. There simply is no place for a woman in the pulpit. It is a stark denial of gender roles to say otherwise.

Yet, many do try to say otherwise. Many churches across the Western world have adopted a pragmatic attitude wherein they attempt to appease and fit in with the world's standards. As feminism has run rampant over secular society, it has slowly encroached the church. Rather than fighting it off, many have been duped into believing the lie that modern man knows better than God. Instead of strongly clinging to the pulpit, men have believed the deception that "Anything a man can do, a woman can do better." The result has been chaos and deterioration.

In fact, one mark of a deteriorating society is sexual decadence, and that always begins with a subversion of the roles of men and women. Consider the wisdom of Italian History Professor Roberto De Mattei who rightly noted that, "The collapse of the Roman Empire and the arrival of the Barbarians was due to the spread of homosexuality.... The Roman colony of Carthage was a paradise for homosexuals and they infected many others."[1] Why was Carthage able to infect others with the sinful spread of homosexuality? Because men were no longer behaving as men within masculine roles. Gender roles were ignored. And we see the same thing happening in many denominations across the West: As soon as gender roles are ignored and women take to the pulpits, it is not long until the rainbow flag flies proudly

---

[1] See Nick Pisa, "Outrage as top Italian history professor blames fall of Rome on rise of homosexuality," Daily Mail, April 8, 2011.

in front of the church to celebrate the LGBTQ+ community.

It was not just the ancient world that suffered from sexual decadence; the medieval world suffered deterioration too when societal roles were ignored. In a chapter aptly titled "The West Torn Apart," Jacques Barzun writes in his work *From Dawn to Decadence* that a major catastrophe facing the West at the turn of the sixteenth century was the inability of society to properly exercise the roles that God had given to govern it. Barzun writes that "Moral turpitude concealed a deeper trouble: the meaning of the roles had been lost. The priest, instead of being a teacher, was ignorant; the monk, instead of helping to save the world by his piety, was an idle profiteer; the bishop, instead of supervising the care of souls in his diocese was a politician and businessman."[2] This created a society that was ripe for Reformation—much like our own day and age as well.

When roles are ignored, anarchy and absurdity are the result. Decadence has come. Barzun

---

[2] Jacques Barzun, *From Dawn to Decadence: 500 Years of Western Cultural Life, 1500 to the Present* (New York, NY: HarperCollins, 2000), 11.

concludes, "When people accept futility and the absurd as normal, the culture is decadent. The term is not a slur; it is a technical label."[3] The Western world in the twenty-first century has not merely accepted the futile and absurd as normal; it has embraced it. The rise of transgenderism has resulted in men entering women's sport competitions and taking the medals to the applause of society. Women have transitioned their appearance into that of men and have been celebrated. And, within the church, women have taken to the pulpit, calling themselves pastors and preachers. These things are all connected, and they are absolutely absurd. Decadence isn't just coming—it's here. It is crouching at the steps of the church and the great danger is that some have already been mastered by it and are trying to let it in.

Make no mistake: This is not a tertiary or even a secondary issue within Christity. Gender roles are of the utmost significance, and the issue of whether or not women should pastor or preach is a primary issue. It is, in fact, the difference between orthodoxy and heterodoxy.

---

[3] Barzun, *Dawn to Decadence*, 11.

The goal of this short work, fundamentally, is to make the biblical and theological case that gender roles matter. More specifically, as a work targeting Christians within the church, this work aims to demonstrate the case that women cannot preach or pastor. They cannot be ordained into ministry. It would be absurd to say any differently because God's Word has specifically prescribed the qualifications of a preacher and pastor and, at the most basic level, a pastor and preacher *must* be a man. There is absolutely no way around this.

A Brief Synopsis of Gender Roles

Yes, gender roles govern the sexes. And that's only possible because God governs His creation.

God created man and woman to rule the earth, fill it, and have dominion over it (Gen. 1:26–28). Within this Dominion Mandate, God further specifies that men are to be workers and keepers (Gen. 2:15). At its most basic level, this means men are to build families, provide for them, and protect them as they spread out across the world for the glory of God. Woman, on the other hand, is created from a rib taken from the side of man (Gen. 2:21–22) and fulfills the role of being his helper (Gen. 2:18).

God's purposes for men and women don't end here, though. He intends for men to marry women, to be fruitful, and to multiply (Gen. 1:28, 2:24). This is part of the way through which dominion of the earth is established. Through the procreation of offspring and the propagation of the gospel, disciples of Christ are made to spread across the earth (Matt. 28:18–20). As the earth is filled with disciples who proclaim the gospel, God's glory spreads, His Kingdom comes, His will is done, and the whole earth continues to be made a footstool beneath the feet of Jesus. And, at the center of this enterprise is the family and the church, where gender roles are vital.

Thus, within creation itself, God reveals fundamental purposes and differences between the sexes that establish their roles. The Apostle Paul further expands on this in Ephesians 5:22–27, wherein he calls for wives to submit to their husbands as unto the Lord, and for husbands to love and lead their wives and children. These gender roles are distinct and important. The husband who is led by his wife is in sin, but so too is the wife who leads her husband.

These roles are neglected at the family's peril, and at the promise of discipline from the Lord.

But it would be a mistake to believe these distinctions end with the household. On the contrary, they expand ever outward. Consider Isaiah 3:12, which states that it is a lamentable thing for a nation to be ruled by women and children. Such texts reveal that society itself is governed by the gender roles that God has established. It is, according to God Himself, lamentable when women rule a nation. Why? Because patriarchy is imbued within the Creation, and something has gone askew when this is not the case.

Think about it. Our Triune God, throughout the Old and New Testaments, is commonly referred to as Father, Son, and Holy Spirit. We, who are created in His image and likeness, inherently know that it is good and right for men, and especially fathers and sons, to lead. Deep down, we know something has gone seriously awry when a woman rules in the place of a man, both in the household and the civil magistrate. Patriarchy is natural and it is good, and mankind, by the grace of God, intuitively knows this.

Of course, if such gender roles extend from the household to society, it is only natural that they would extend further into the ecclesiastical order of the church at large. The descriptions of 1 Timothy 3 and Titus 1 use exclusively masculine language when speaking of the leaders of the church. Men are elders; men are deacons; men are called by God to preach and teach His Word. Women? Not so much. Men are to lead within the church, while women are to submit to the rule of those men who have been placed in charge over them. The only ones arguing differently are those who are in sin.

All this to say, at the most basic level: Sally can't preach.

Looking Ahead

This short work will follow a very simple plan. To explain *why* women cannot preach or pastor, we will examine Scripture to make a thoroughly biblical, theological, and doctrinal argument in chapters 1 and 2. Following this, in chapters 3 and 4, we will ex-amine some historical considerations and recent de-velopments that have necessitated the writing of this work. Chapter 5 will then model how biblically faith-ful Christians must fight this war of gender roles with the truth of Scripture on their side.

This will not be a long work, and that's primarily for two reasons: 1. It doesn't have to be. While we could wax and wane elegantly about the whole debate, the truth is that Scripture is cut and dry on the matter. 2. I desire this to be readable and to reach as wide an audience as possible; even those who disagree. My goal is both persuasion and reinforcement. I wish to persuade those who believe women can preach or pastor to instead understand that it is sinful for women to try to do so. I also hope to encourage those who already hold to the orthodox position that women cannot preach or pastor to continue holding to that position. The enemy may march against us, but we have both the Lord and His inspired Word on our side.

May God bless this work and lead those who read it into the truth of His Word.

1

A Gender War

Thomas "Stonewall" Jackson once stood in the Shenandoah Valley and surveyed the grounds where a Civil War battle had only recently taken place. Turning to an aide, he asked, "Did you ever think, sir, what an opportunity a battlefield affords liars?"[1] What he meant, of course, was that times of war are the ripe play fields of liars. They can deceive on the battlefield in order to gain the upper hand, or, should they win the battle, they can turn their lies into legends believed by the masses. As the saying goes, "History is written by the victors."

This is incredibly important for Christians to understand today as the church finds itself amid a battle for the sexes. Like those raising the Tower of Babel in defiance to God, modern man raises his gender-confused idols to openly defy God's design and

[1] James I. Robertson, *Stonewall Jackson: The Man, The Soldier, The Legend* (New York: Macmillan Publishing Co, 1997), x.

purposefully determined gender roles. Even within the church, there is a war being waged between those who hold to Scripture and its defined gender roles and those who wish to throw the Bible from their fast-moving cars in favor of adopting pragmatic and fluid philosophies for the genders. One battle being waged within this war is attempting to determine whether women can be ordained into ministry to preach and pastor.

Now, in a battle, there will be those who are fighting for the truth and those who are fighting against the truth. Those fighting against the truth will lie, deceive, and delude as many as they can to try and win. This is exactly what proponents of women in ministry are doing: they are attempting to twist Scripture, appeal to emotions, hold up their own past accomplishments, and bamboozle the masses into believing the lie that women can preach or pastor. It's like the magician's sleight of hand: they turn our attention away from the Scriptures and toward themselves so that we may not see what they are really doing and so be more easily deceived. But as followers of Christ and His Word, we are followers of the Truth (John 8:32, 14:6) and must employ only the Truth of Scripture in our battle.

Tearing Down Arguments and Lofty Opinions Against God

Deceptions, emotional appeals, and the twisting of Scripture are sinful tactics that the faithful Christian must never utilize in battle. In fact, the church is to act as "a pillar and buttress of the truth" (1 Tim. 3:15), and as Christians within the church, Christ has equipped us with weapons that are far different than anything else found in this world. As Paul explains in 2 Corinthians 10:4–6:

> For the weapons of our warfare are not of the flesh but have divine power to destroy strongholds. We destroy arguments and every lofty opinion raised against the knowledge of God, and take every thought captive to obey Christ, being ready to punish every disobedience, when your obedience is complete.

The question for the Christian battling against this heretical practice of women in ministry is simply this: How do we employ the truth to do righteous battle in the gender war? How do we destroy the arguments and lofty opinions that argue that women are permitted to preach and pastor and be ordained? How do we effectively punish disobedience?

To answer these questions, we must always keep in the forefront of our minds that the weapon Christ has given to us is none other than His Word. Consider how Christ Himself, when He inevitably and finally returns to this earth in triumphant victory, will come to conquer the nations with only His Word: "From his mouth comes a sharp sword with which to strike down the nations, and he will rule them with a rod of iron. He will tread the winepress of the fury of the wrath of God the Almighty" (Rev. 19:15). Likewise, consider how Jesus knocked His enemies to the ground simply by speaking to them when they came to arrest Him without cause: "When Jesus said to them, 'I am he,' they drew back and fell to the ground" (John 18:6). Of course, Jesus defeated Satan and temptations by quoting Scripture (Matt. 4:1–11). Finally, consider how God's Word holds the very power of life and creation: "By the word of the Lord the heavens were made, and by the breath of his mouth all their host.... For he spoke, and it came to be; he commanded, and it stood firm" (Ps. 33:6, 9). God does battle with the truth of His Word because

His enemies always crumple when confronted with it. That's the power of His Word.

This same power is ours to wield through His Word. If we desire to cut down those lofty arguments and conquer the strongholds that have taken people captive, that they might instead become captives of Christ alone, then the greatest weapons in our arsenal are the Word of God and prayer. Through these twin swords, we can cut down the enemy's arguments and call down fire from Heaven so that Christ's enemies will be conquered, either through repentance and salvation, or through judgment and damnation.

Similarly, disobedience is punished through the Word. Not only can we proclaim the truth that those who deny Christ and His Word will be judged, but we can also follow Jesus's own commandments regarding church discipline (Matt. 18:15–20, 1 Cor. 5:1–13) when it comes to dealing with those within our own fellowship who deny God's design for the sexes.

None of this is ever to be done in an angry or vengeful spirit, though. Rather, out of love for God, His Word, and concern for those who are in sin, we proclaim and live by the truth of God's Word and openly call sinners to repentance.

Some may perhaps ask, at this point, whether a denial of gender roles is worthy of church discipline, and it is a good question. I believe it is a case worthy of church discipline *if* the gender roles have been properly explained from Scripture and the church member in question continues to act defiantly against God's commands. A new Christian may simply misunderstand and need to have these things explained to them. If we find such a one in our churches who believes that Sally can and should preach, we should go and speak with them. Reason with them from the Scriptures. If they will not repent, we ought to involve the elders. If still they will not repent, the matter ought to be taken before the church and, if repentance still does not follow, then their membership is to be revoked, their access to the Lord's Table removed, and we are to treat them as an unbeliever. At the same time, the church ought to continue to pray earnestly for their repentance and restoration to the fellowship.

According to God's Word, we punish their disobedience with church discipline. Though this may seem harsh to many, we must reiterate at this point that this is no tertiary or secondary matter. The issue of who may and who may not inhabit the pulpit is a primary matter and concern of the church. To deny gender roles in the pulpit is to deny God's good design in creation. Our churches, according to God's Word, need to take this matter as seriously as God does.

The Divine Power of the Scriptures

Again, the Christian's main source of truth and divine power comes from the Scriptures, for it is there that the Christian meets with the very Word of God. And, as it turns out, Scripture has much to say about the qualifications of the one in ministry.

Perhaps the most well-known text regarding ministerial qualifications is found in 1 Timothy 3:1–7. Consider the following:

> The saying is trustworthy: If anyone aspires to the office of overseer, *he* desires a noble task. Therefore an overseer must be above reproach, the *husband* of one wife, sober-minded, self-controlled, respectable, hospitable, able to teach, not a drunkard, not violent but gentle, not quarrelsome, not a lover of money. *He* must manage *his* own household well, with all dignity keeping *his*

> children submissive, for if someone does not know how to manage *his* own household, how will *he* care for God's church? *He* must not be a recent convert, or *he* may become puffed up with conceit and fall into the condemnation of the devil. Moreover, *he* must be well thought of by outsiders, so that *he* may not fall into disgrace, into a snare of the devil. (Italics my own for emphasis.)

Within this text, outlining the qualifications for an overseer (another name for elder or pastor), we see that strictly masculine language is employed. Eleven times in seven verses, masculine pronouns are used to describe the one seeking such office. Feminine pronouns are never utilized. Clearly, if the Holy Spirit had intended for Christians to know that women could pastor too, He would have inspired Paul to enlist a different choice of wording. Instead, the Holy Spirit inspired Paul to list very particular *masculine* qualifications for a pastor.

If that remains unconvincing, then the fact that an overseer/elder/pastor must be the *husband* of one wife should settle the matter. Can a woman become the husband of a wife? Though the world may say differently, God's Word clearly states that gender is not fluid, and a woman can only ever rightfully be the wife of one man. A woman can never become a husband.

Furthermore, in 1 Timothy 2:12 Paul sets up the requirements for eldership in chapter 3 by first plainly stating that, "I do not permit a woman to teach or to exercise authority over a man; rather, she is to remain quiet." And, just in case one desires to ignore this statement by arguing that this was purely a cultural concern for Timothy's congregation in Ephesus, 1 Corinthians 14:33–34[2] states much the same. Women were not permitted to preach or hold authority over men in any congregation of the early church. Why? Because God established men to lead women (1 Timothy 2:13–14).

Let's consider these things in greater depth.

---

[2] "For God is not a God of confusion but of peace. *As in all the churches of the saints,* the women should keep silent in the churches. For they are not permitted to speak, but should be in submission, as the Law also says." Emphasis my own. Paul clearly would not have emphasized this as a practice in *all the churches* if this was not genuinely practiced in all churches.

God created men and women to serve *complementary* roles within the home, church, and society.

Consider the way Paul's arguments precede his commandments regarding elders in 1 Timothy 2:8–10:

> I desire then that in every place the men should pray, lifting holy hands without anger or quarreling; likewise also that women should adorn themselves in respectable apparel, with modesty and self-control, not with braided hair and gold or pearls or costly attire, but with what is proper for women who profess godliness—with good works.

Is Paul saying that men are greater than women? Of course not. Is he saying that women cannot do anything at all? Again, this is clearly not the case. But compared to our modern society, Paul does subvert quite a few of our expectations.

Paul first emphasizes that Christian men should be men of prayer. Yet, how many men do you know that are actually known to be men of prayer? The popular nomenclature for saints who are known to pray often is "Prayer Warrior." So, how many *male* prayer warriors do you know?

My own experience growing up was that it was almost always exclusively the women who were blatantly referred to as "Prayer Warriors." Typically, if something was wrong, it was the women who said they were praying for you in church. The pastor would pray, of course, and perhaps a few men would be called upon throughout the church service, but throughout the week, the women were the ones known to be praying. Of course, women *should* pray, but it is to the shame of men when women are known to be *greater* warriors of prayer than they are. While it is true that Sally cannot preach, and that she should not lead public prayer in a corporate assembly, it is also true that men need to take their posts. If we will follow Scripture in not allowing Sally to preach, then the men must be faithful to *do* what God's Word requires. Men must pray. They must not be angry or quarrelsome, but faithful to pray and praise God.

Well, then, how do women fit into this? Men pave the way by their own leadership and example and then women come in as the help-meets. Notice how important the commandments for women are:

They are to dress respectably in modest apparel, exercise self-control, and perform good works. Clearly, then, there are things that a woman can do within church. Paul summarizes her work in Titus 2:3–5:

> Older women likewise are to be reverent in behavior, not slanderers or slaves to much wine. They are to teach what is good, and so train the young women to love their husbands and children, to be self-controlled, pure, working at home, kind, and submissive to their own husbands, that the word of God may not be reviled.

Yes, the men are to lead. But the women serve very specific functions that the men cannot fulfill. The good works of the faithful woman are the training of young women to love their husbands and submit to them and to love their children. Women are to teach other women how to be self-controlled and pure (not given to sin, but righteous and holy), how to faithfully work at home, and how to be kind. Through all of this, the Christian woman's task is to make sure that God's Word is not reviled.

So, a woman can teach other women. She can teach children. She must teach her own children. Far from being unimportant, her work greatly complements the work of her husband and other men who lead the church. Her *complementary* work causes the Body of Christ at large to become most productive and fruitful for God's Kingdom. Adam could not effectively operate without Eve, and men absolutely need women in their service to the Lord. God has intentionally designed the sexes in this way.

Women are not *ever* permitted to teach or hold authority over men in church.

Paul could not possibly be any clearer on this matter than he is in 1 Timothy 2:11–12: "Let a woman learn quietly with all submissiveness. I do not permit a woman to teach or to exercise authority over a man; rather, she is to remain quiet."

Women are to learn *quietly*. The very fact that she is to be *quiet* prohibits her from teaching or preaching. Obviously, the woman who teaches or preaches is not quiet, and is thus sinning against God and His Word.

Does this mean she can never speak? Of course not. She must lift her voice in praise to God during the worship, in harmony with the other saints. She can ask her pastor questions after the service. She can ask her husband questions on the ride home from church. She can discuss the sermon with her husband, children, and friends. The call to be silent is within the context of teaching or leading during a worship service.

Now, there may be some who would then venture forth with this claim: "If she's to be quiet during the preaching, there is at least room for her to teach during the Sunday School hour." Again, however, Scripture is quite clear: She cannot exercise authority over men. She must remain quiet and not teach. To stand behind a pulpit or teach the men of the church from God's Word, at any point in the church's corporate gathering, is wrong.

Some may question, "Can a woman ever share the gospel with a man, then?" She can, but there is great wisdom in her husband being with her and leading the charge. This is what the Scriptures reveal in Acts 18:24–28, wherein Priscilla is with her husband Aquilla, and together they proclaim the fullness of the gospel to Apollos. This is how women can most effectively help their husbands in gospel work.

However, to reiterate, there is no issue with a woman teaching other women without her husband present, nor is there an issue with her teaching her children without her husband present (though he should be, if possible).

There is also wisdom in considering her age when it comes to teaching the youth of a church: Can she effectively speak to little boys as a mother would her sons, or is she too young to do so? Outside of nursery environments (where it is assuredly best to have women present to care for the children), great caution must be exercised when it comes to women teaching teens. In this area, I think it best to insist that faithful men also engage in the teaching of the children within the church, lest little boys mature into young men who are still under the authority of a woman as their Sunday School teacher. This, after all, would be sinful. When boys become men, they must no longer be under the authority of a woman during Sunday School.

God's order of creation established the roles of men and women.

Husbands leading with their wives submitting to them and supporting them is simply imbued within God's created order. There is no escaping it. In fact, the entire basis of Paul's argument for men and women *is* creation itself. First Timothy 2:13–15: "For Adam was formed first, then Eve; and Adam was not deceived, but the woman was deceived and became a transgressor. Yet she will be saved through childbearing—if they continue in faith and love and holiness, with self-control."

One of the arguments that have been employed against Paul's strict commandments for women is that he was writing to Christians within a male-dominated culture. Women were not taught to read, write, or orate. Therefore, it was unsafe for them to teach. So, those in favor of Sally preaching ultimately argue that if women would have been trained as the men were, and if they could have *effectively* taught as the men did, then Paul would have permitted it. Ultimately, according to this line of argumentation, modern woman is more than capable of teaching since she is just as learned as the men around her, if not more so, and thus even the Apostle Paul would have no trouble permitting her to the pulpit today. But that argument completely falls apart once Paul's *actual* argument is considered.

Sally cannot preach because God created Adam first, then Eve. Sally cannot preach because it was

Eve who was first deceived and became a transgressor. No, Sally most assuredly cannot preach, but through Christ she is saved, and through childbearing, faith, love, holiness, and self-control, she is sanctified in Christ.

Paul's entire argument is based upon the order of God's creation in Genesis 2 and then man's fall into sin in Genesis 3. This is part of what makes the entire argument so very important. If Paul's argumentation is objected to and denied, then Genesis must also be rejected. And, if Genesis is rejected, then the very first book of the Bible, and the foundation for God's plan of salvation and Christ's redemptive work, is lost.

Now, if all Paul had said was, "I do not permit a woman to hold authority over men because Adam was created first," then that would have been enough. From the account in Genesis, it is abundantly clear that man is created to lead, and woman is created to submit to man and help him in his God-given calling and vocation. But Paul makes his argument even more powerful by bringing the Fall into account. It is as though Paul is saying, "Man was created first and therefore must lead. There is, however, something that woman was first in, and that was in being deceived by the Serpent to become a transgressor." This is not at all saying that woman is less intelligent than man or that she is lesser in some way when compared to man. This is simply a declaration of truth: Because of Eve, woman has fallen into sin just like man has. Though it is now the woman's desire to usurp authority from men (Gen. 3:16), she simply cannot be permitted to do so.

Throughout most of church history, Paul's commandments here were received as the authoritative Word of God because that's exactly what they are. Having been commissioned by Jesus Christ Himself to become an Apostle, Paul's writings are to be received just as authoritatively as we do all the other words of Scripture, recognizing that they are inspired by the Holy Spirit. Review just about any commentary within the orthodox Christian tradition, and the commentator will agree wholeheartedly and unreservedly with Paul's words. For example, John Calvin's commentary on this text is incredibly insightful. He wrote:

> Not that he takes from them the charge of instructing their family, but only excludes them from the office of teaching, which God has

committed to men only. On this subject we have explained our views in the exposition of the First Epistle to the Corinthians. If any one bring forward, by way of objection, Deborah (Judges 4:4) and others of the same class, of whom we read that they were at one time appointed by the command of God to govern the people, the answer is easy. Extraordinary acts done by God do not overturn the ordinary rules of government, by which he intended that we should be bound. Accordingly, if women at one time held the office of prophets and teachers, and that too when they were supernaturally called to it by the Spirit of God, He who is above all law might do this; but, being a peculiar case, this is not opposed to the constant and ordinary system of government....

What is closely allied to the office of teaching—and not to assume authority over the man; for the very reason, why they are forbidden to teach, is, that it is not permitted by their condition. They are subject, and to teach implies the rank of power or authority. Yet it may be thought that there is no great force in this argument; because even prophets and teachers are subject to kings and to other magistrates. I reply, there is

> no absurdity in the same person commanding and likewise obeying, when viewed in different relations. But this does not apply to the case of woman, who by nature (that is, by the ordinary law of God) is formed to obey; for *gunaikokratia* (the government of women) has always been regarded by all wise persons as a monstrous thing; and, therefore, so to speak, it will be a mingling of heaven and earth, if women usurp the right to teach. Accordingly, he bids them be "quiet," that is, keep within their own rank.[3]

Woman has a rank. Man has a rank. Both have been given their ranks by God. It is essential that man and woman stay within those ranks to honor the Lord.

---

[3] John Calvin, *Commentaries on the Epistles to Timothy, Titus, and Philemon*, trans. Rev. William Pringle (Edinburgh, Scotland: Calvin Translation Society, 1856), 67–68.

2

Biblical Qualification

Abraham Kuyper was almost eerily prophetic when, during his famous 1898 *Lectures on Calvinism*, he stated that, "Finally Modernism, which denies and abolishes every difference, cannot rest until it has made woman man and man woman, and, putting every distinction on a common level, kills life by placing it under the ban of uniformity."[1] This is exactly what modernism has tried to do. It has attempted to kill the distinctions between men and women. It has tried, ultimately, to put Sally in the pulpit.

One of the great problems with postmodernist thought is that it is anti-rule and anti-order. Rather than submit to anything as authoritative, it seeks to undermine all things that are objectively true by appealing instead to the subjective whims and fancies

[1] Abraham Kuyper, *Lectures on Calvinism* (New York, NY: Cosimo Books, 2007), 27.

of men and women. In other words, those in favor of Sally preaching will often argue something like this: "It doesn't matter what Scripture says. Sally sincerely desires to preach, and so she should be permitted into the pulpit." What this argument fails to consider is the fact that that even the sincere can be wrong and sinners are often *sincerely* wrong. A general *feeling* of sincerity is no mark of truth or qualification. In fact, and unsurprisingly, *feelings* are not mentioned in Paul's list of qualifications for elders and deacons in 1 Timothy 3.

Qualifications for Elders

Context is key, and Christ is King. What that means for the interpreter of Scripture is that we must recognize Christ's Word is always authoritative, binding, and true, and in order to fully understand it, it must be read in its proper context. This means that the interpreter must recognize that the elder's qualifications listed in 1 Timothy 3 are right, true, and good, but they do not occur within a remote vacuum. Rather, the qualifications are listed *after* the prohibitions against women holding a position of authority over men and after Paul has explicitly stated that women are not permitted to teach men within corporate gatherings.

When chapter 3 begins, Paul is still dealing with the same theme of who the proper teachers of God's Word are to be. Thus, he writes in verses 1–7:

> The saying is trustworthy: If anyone aspires to the office of overseer, he desires a noble task. Therefore an overseer must be above reproach, the husband of one wife, sober-minded, self-controlled, respectable, hospitable, able to teach, not a drunkard, not violent but gentle, not quarrelsome, not a lover of money. He must manage his own household well, with all dignity keeping his children submissive, for if someone does not know how to manage his own household, how will he care for God's church? He must not be a recent convert, or he may become puffed up with conceit and fall into the condemnation of the devil. Moreover, he must be well thought of by outsiders, so that he may not fall into disgrace, into a snare of the devil.

As previously stated, Paul uses eleven masculine pronouns within seven verses to describe the proper candidates for eldership. After studying 1 Timothy 2:15–17, there can be no mistaking Paul's intentions in the text of 1 Timothy 3:1–7: Women are prohibited from seeking eldership, and churches are prohibited from ordaining women into eldership. It is a denial of God's Word and, therefore, sinful to think or do otherwise. Either God's Word must be upheld, or entirely rejected.

To be sure, not every man is called to the role of elder. It is a noble and high calling. In fact, Paul describes a trustworthy saying when he states that the role of an elder is a noble one. He is still trustworthy when he describes the list of qualifications for elders. Lest any men reading this fail to take into account just how high of a calling this is, and how serious it is, let's consider the following qualifications:

1. An elder must be above reproach.
2. An elder must be the husband of one wife.
3. An elder must be sober-minded.
4. An elder must be self-controlled.
5. An elder must be respectable.
6. An elder must be hospitable.
7. An elder must be able to teach.
8. An elder must not be a drunkard.

9. An elder must not be violent.
10. An elder must be gentle.
11. An elder must not be quarrelsome.
12. An elder must not be a lover of money.
13. An elder must be one who manages his household well with dignity.
14. An elder must not be a recent convert.
15. An elder must be thought of well by outsiders.

James, of course, was right when he plainly stated that, “Not many of you should become teachers, my brothers, for you know that we who teach will be judged with greater strictness” (James 3:1). Not every man is qualified for this role. Absolutely no woman is qualified for this role. If the man who is unqualified is going to be severely judged for taking this role, how much more severe will be the judgment upon the woman who steps into the role of elder?

Out of love and by way of warning, it is only right that a call of repentance be placed here: If the one reading this is an unqualified man serving as an elder, then you must repent and immediately step down from the role. It is best for you and the church.

If the one reading this is a woman serving in the capacity of elder, then you must repent and immediately step down from that role. If the one reading this is a member of a church that is "pastored" by a woman, then you must repent and immediately leave that church. It is better that "Ichabod" be written above the doors of the church and that its doors permanently close than you waste any more time there.

Qualifications for Deacons

After outlining the qualifications for elders, Paul immediately begins discussing the qualifications for deacons in 1 Timothy 3:8–13:

> Deacons likewise must be dignified, not double-tongued, not addicted to much wine, not greedy for dishonest gain. They must hold the mystery of the faith with a clear conscience. And let them also be tested first; then let them serve as deacons if they prove themselves blameless. Their wives likewise must be dignified, not slanderers, but sober-minded, faithful in all things. Let deacons each be the husband of one wife, managing

> their children and their own households well. For those who serve well as deacons gain a good standing for themselves and also great confidence in the faith that is in Christ Jesus.

The most difficult part about explaining this text is not interpreting what Paul is saying but explaining what a deacon does. This is because many churches mean something quite different when they speak of deacons. Thus, some definition is necessary here to distinguish a deacon from an elder. A deacon (Greek, *diakonos*) is one who serves. This is different from an elder (Greek, *episkopos*), which refers to one who is an overseer and judge. In fact, in Greek, the word for *elder* is closely linked to God's Day of visitation and judgment, as in 1 Peter 2:12, wherein Peter wrote, "Keep your conduct among the Gentiles honorable, so that when they speak against you as evildoers, they may see your good deeds and glorify God on the day of visitation." The word translated, "of visitation," is the Greek *episkopēs*, revealing that there is a large connection between the elder and a "visiting judge."

For a clear distinction between an elder and deacon, consider Acts 6:1–7:

Now in these days when the disciples were increasing in number, a complaint by the Hellenists arose against the Hebrews because their widows were being neglected in the daily distribution. And the twelve summoned the full number of the disciples and said, "It is not right that we should give up preaching the word of God to serve tables. Therefore, brothers, pick out from among you seven men of good repute, full of the Spirit and of wisdom, whom we will appoint to this duty. But we will devote ourselves to prayer and to the ministry of the word." And what they said pleased the whole gathering, and they chose Stephen, a man full of faith and of the Holy Spirit, and Philip, and Prochorus, and Nicanor, and Timon, and Parmenas, and Nicolaus, a proselyte of Antioch. These they set before the apostles, and they prayed and laid their hands on them.

And the word of God continued to increase, and the number of the disciples multiplied greatly in Jerusalem, and a great many of the priests became obedient to the faith.

Within this text, we see that the twelve were serving as elders. They were faithfully preaching the Word of God, but their effectiveness to do so was threatened by the problems piling up within the church. So, they gathered the people together to find seven faithful *men* who would be able to meet the need of *waiting tables*. While the deacons served in this capacity, the elders would lead and oversee the congregation by giving themselves entirely over to prayer and the ministry of the Word.

So, with that in mind, it's time for the million-dollar question: Can women serve as deacons? Let's consider the qualifications:

1. Deacons must be dignified.
2. Deacons must not be double-tongued.
3. Deacons must not be addicted to wine.
4. Deacons must not be greedy for dishonest gain.
5. Deacons must be faithful to the gospel (the mystery of the faith).
6. Deacons must be clear in the conscience.
7. Deacons must be first tested and proved blameless.
8. Deacons' wives must be dignified.

9. Deacons' wives must not be slanderers.
10. Deacons' wives must be sober-minded.
11. Deacons' wives must be faithful in all things.
12. Deacons must be the husband of one wife.
13. Deacons must be good managers of their own households.

There is, unsurprisingly, some overlap between the qualifications for elders and deacons. Deacons may not be leaders, but they do hold a position of some authority and influence within the church congregation. What is different between the two lists is that qualifications are listed for deacons' wives, whereas there are no such qualifications placed upon the wives of elders. Thus, some argue that women should be permitted to become deacons. They would agree wholeheartedly that Sally cannot preach, but that Sally can serve as a *deaconess*.

I do not deny the idea that it is possible for a wife to help her husband serve as a deacon. In fact, I think this is right and good. After all, if a widow or other woman in the church is in need of some help, a man should bring his wife along with him, lest any word of reproach be spoken against him by outsiders and lest he fall into any sort of temptation himself. In fact, this is likely the exact reason Paul brings up deacons' wives: There was an expectation that, as her husband's helper, a wife would support her husband's work as a deacon. On the other hand, a wife is to support her husband's work as an elder too, but she cannot enter the pulpit to help him teach. The two roles are distinctly different.

It is the twelfth qualification, however, that seals the deal: Sally cannot be commissioned as a deacon because a deacon must also be the husband of one wife. Can Sally serve at all, however? Of course! While she cannot hold to the office of deacon within the church, she can most certainly serve the Body of Christ, the poor, the needy, and especially her husband and children.

Phoebe is the perfect example of this. In Romans 16:1–2, Paul writes, "I commend to you our sister Phoebe, a servant of the church at Cenchreae, that you may welcome her in the Lord in a way worthy of the saints, and help her in whatever she may need from you, for she has been a patron of many and of myself as well." In Greek, the word that has been translated servant is the word *diakanon*, which is related to the word deacon. However, this does not mean that Phoebe held to the office of deacon; rather, it means that she *served* the Body of Christ in the ways that a woman is permitted to serve. She was a *patron* both of Paul and of others, which means she supported Paul in the work of the ministry and helped others where she could. Perhaps this means she financially supported the work of the ministry, or fed Paul, or prayed on behalf of Paul and others. Whatever the case, Phoebe was commended by the same Paul who wrote 1 Timothy 2 and 3. It can be deduced that she faithfully served as a woman should and did not sinfully attempt to usurp a position of power or role of authority she was not meant to bear. When rightfully understood, Phoebe becomes a godly model for all women to imitate.

In short, both the qualifications for elders and deacons prohibit Sally from serving within them. She is not prohibited from serving Christ and His Body in various other capacities, but the roles of elder and deacon are reserved for biblically qualified men alone.

3

The Battle Lines Drawn

In 2019, John MacArthur sent shockwaves throughout evangelicalism when, during Grace Community Church's *Truth Matters Conference,* he was asked about "women preachers" like Beth Moore. Specifically, he was asked to respond to Beth Moore and her apparent appetite to become a pastor and preacher. MacArthur's response was simple enough: "Go home."[1]

Shocked and awed gasps were heard across the frontlines of evangelicalism. People quite simply could not understand how MacArthur could say such a "terrible" thing to Beth Moore. "How

---

[1] Leonardo Blair, "John MacArthur skewers Beth Moore, Paula White, evangelicals who support women preachers," *The Christian Post,* October 21, 2019 (https://www.christianpost.com/news/john-macarthur-skewers-beth-moore-paula-white-evangelicals-who-support-women-preachers.html).

degrading!" Some said. "How belittling!" It was simply unthinkable to a postmodern and egalitarian church world that a woman could possibly be told that her rightful place was in the home and not in the pulpit.

MacArthur was not wrong for what he said. In fact, I contend that his response to Beth Moore was even more gracious than most would have you believe. After all, the woman of Proverbs 31:10–31 is described as an excellent woman and wife, and she is a woman who is never in the pulpit but works at home. She is more precious than jewels (v. 10) because "The heart of her husband trusts in her, and he will have no lack of gain" (v. 11). The reason her husband can trust her is because "She seeks wool and flax, and works with willing hands" (v. 12). She is industrious. Rising while it is night, she "provides food for her household and portions for her maidens" (v. 15). She purchases and plants fields (v. 16), dresses herself and her family (vv. 17, 21), gives to the poor (v. 20), and is the helpmeet that her husband most desperately needs (v. 23). She fears nothing of the future for her household because she has not been idle but has continually worked to make a home for her family. Her husband and children praise her before leaders

(vv. 28–29) and her own works bring her praise before others (v. 31). She has great value and worth to her husband, children, and the world precisely because she works in her home.

The simple truth is this: Beth Moore's rightful place *is* in the home, caring for her family. That's the rightful place of all women. The pulpit, however, is not a woman's home. It is the sacred desk of biblically qualified men from whence the Word of God is to be faithfully exposited and proclaimed. Any woman who attempts to stand behind the sacred desk must graciously be told exactly what MacArthur told Moore: Go home. Your rightful place is there, submitting to the rule of your husband and providing nurture and care for your family.

Perhaps some are confused because they believe that the position makes the person. They may be confused because they believe that, since Scripture plainly declares women cannot preach or pastor, that conservative Christians must think women to be lesser than men. On the contrary. The position and the role *do not* make the person. Positions don't make people more powerful. Roles don't make people more important. In a sense, people make the roles and positions they fulfill and, according to God, women simply cannot fulfill the role of pastor or preacher, any more than a man can fulfill the role of mother. It is because we hold both genders in high esteem that we simply cannot allow violence to be done to God's Creation or His Word by the upheaval of normative gender roles within the church.

A Downward Spiral

The issue does not end with Beth Moore. Consider one Aimee Byrd, once an apparent defender of gender roles. At one point, she claimed that it was not right for women to take to the pulpits or to seek ordination as pastors. Yet, even in 2013, when defending complementarianism (the belief that the roles of men and women are different and yet complementary, in that men are to lead and women are to submit to their husband's rule), she made certain statements that should have raised red flags. In one blog post, she wrote:

> Could I compose and deliver a sermon-worthy exposition of Scripture that would enlighten

> those listening? Sure I could, along with many other women. But this is not our calling...[2]

Do pay close attention to what she was saying. Even as she claimed that women were not to preach because God had not given them that calling, she did think that women *could* preach. There is a problem with such thinking because it reveals a terrible misunderstanding of what preaching is. Preaching is not just composing and delivering an exposition of Scripture; preaching is, as Martyn Lloyd-Jones famously said, "Logic on fire." Behind powerful preaching is the Holy Spirit giving unction, passion, tenacity, wisdom, and power. The reason why a woman not only *should not* preach but *cannot* preach is because the Holy Spirit is not going to equip someone to do something He has not called them to do. He is not the author of confusion (1 Cor. 14:33).

If, as Aimee Byrd claimed, she had been capable of composing and delivering an exposition of

---

[2] Aimee Byrd, "What's the Difference Between Women Preaching and Women Blogging?," *Reformation 21*, September 11, 2013 (https://www.reformation21.org/mos/housewife-theologian/whats-the-difference-between-women-preaching-and-women-blogging).

Scripture, then it would not have been by the power of the Holy Spirit. Rather, such ability would either come from the self—and thus would not be true preaching—or would be fueled by the spirit of anti-christ.

When the Apostle John wrote to Christians to beware of false prophets, one of the distinguishing marks he warned against was that they would be loved by the world. "They are from the world; therefore they speak from the world, and the world listens to them" (1 John 4:5). Those who claim women should and can preach or pastor are, unsurprisingly, loved by the world. A gender confused society absolutely loves to embrace egalitarians and soft-complementarians because their theology of the sexes lines up with the world's own view of gender roles. We must guard against such novelties in our churches and pulpits.

Byrd was not done with her comments, however. Notice the subtle argument she employs next:

> So as for men not learning from women, this has to do with the authority of the position of an elder. Outside of this, we are foolish to think that men do not learn from women. How can we be

> helpers if we are not all teachers of some sort? And with all the influence that women do have in the church, the home, and the world, we should want them to be very good theologians.[3]

The basic idea and implication here is that because *everyone is a theologian*, women must have *some* opportunity and capacity to teach men spiritual things. To think otherwise would be "foolish." Does any Christian truly deny this? Of course not. The same God who can speak and teach adults through the mouth of babes is most certainly capable of teaching through the mouth of women. The difference is that women cannot ever teach from the pulpit, or preach, or hold authority over men. Thus, that means women cannot teach Sunday School, preach a sermon, hold worship, lead corporate prayer, and so on. But Byrd's trajectory was already set and fast forward about a decade later, and the theological drift is openly on display. In 2022, Byrd "preached" her first

---

[3] Byrd, "What's the Difference?"

Sunday morning sermon during a church's worship service.[4]

What happened? The spirit of antichrist was finally revealed. As John warns in 1 John 4:1–3:

> Beloved, do not believe every spirit, but test the spirits to see whether they are from God, for many false prophets have gone out into the world. By this you know the Spirit of God: every spirit that confesses that Jesus Christ has come in the flesh is from God, and every spirit that does not confess Jesus is not from God. This is the spirit of the antichrist, which you heard was coming and now is in the world already.

And, again, in 1 John 2:18–19, he warned Christians to be ready for this very hour:

> Children, it is the last hour, and as you have heard that antichrist is coming, so now many antichrists have come. Therefore we know that it is

---

[4] Colin Smothers, "That Was Then, This Is Now: Aimee Byrd Preaches Her First Sunday Morning Sermon," *The Council on Biblical Manhood and Womanhood*, March 9, 2022 (https://cbmw.org/2022/03/09/that-was-then-this-is-now-aimee-byrd-preaches-her-first-sunday-morning-sermon/).

> the last hour. They went out from us, but they were not of us; for if they had been of us, they would have continued with us. But they went out, that it might become plain that they all are not of us.

By denying God's purposefully designed gender roles for the church, which have been imbued in His creation itself, Byrd denied God's order in creation. By stepping behind a sacred desk to "preach," she was denying God's Word. By denying God's Word, she effectively denied Christ. By denying Christ, she has revealed the spirit of antichrist within. This antichristological spirit both stands in opposition against Christ and His Word and attempts to set itself up in place of Christ and His Word. It openly defies Him and seeks the adoration, respect, reverence, and praise that is due to Him alone.

The good news, for all redeemed saints, is that, "Little children, you are from God and have overcome them, for he who is in you is greater than he who is in the world" (1 John 4:5). Try as they may, egalitarians, soft-complementarians, and feminist proponents of women in the pulpit cannot erase God's Word. Sally still can't preach.

A Nebuchadnezzar-like Defense

While we could devote much more time to tracing the history of the Byrds and Moores of evangelicalism, it is worth noting that certain men have also become proponents of women in the pulpit. They have, perhaps, committed the worse sin. Rather than leading these women down the path of repentance, they have taken their hands to walk in sin alongside them.

These men are like the charlatans of the old west; snake-oil salesman who have both been deceived and seek to deceive others. The men who defend women in ministry are effeminate and hardly worth calling men at all. Rather than lead, they have cowardly submitted to the women around them.

One such proponent of women in ministry is the well-known Rick Warren, author of *The Purpose Driven Life* and former pastor of Saddleback Church—one of the largest churches in the United States and formerly part of the Southern Baptist Convention. What makes his defense of women in leadership particularly egregious is that he has spent literal decades in ministry, preached many sermons (which, one would assume, required much time of study in the Scriptures), and is well-acquainted with the Southern Baptist Convention's statements of belief and confessions. In other words, he should know better.

The Southern Baptist Confession is quite concise on the matter. Within the *Baptist Faith and Message 2000* the following, straightforward statement is included: "Its [the church's] scriptural officers are pastors and deacons. While both men and women are gifted for service in the church, the office of pastor is limited to men as qualified by Scripture."[5] This is incredibly simple. The office of pastor, and therefore preacher, is only permitted to be filled by *men*.

Over the years, Rick Warren has basically ignored these sacred and foundational truths. He has ordained women into eldership and has appointed a man and woman to pastor the church upon his retirement as a husband-and-wife team. Unsurprisingly, many called for his removal from the SBC, but he would be allowed a defense. So, when it finally came time to make his defense and he stood before the Southern Baptist Convention in 2022, he had a chance to make a biblical argument for his beliefs.

---

[5] The Baptist Faith and Message 2000, Section VI.

So, why did he believe that women could now pastor and preach? Here's his defense:

> I preached over 120 harvest crusades before I was twenty, we baptized 56,631 new believers, sent 20,869 members overseas to 197 nations, 78,157 members of our church signed our membership covenant, I had the privilege of training over 1.1 million pastors. Sorry friends, that's more than all of our seminaries put together...[6]

Rather than making a biblical or theological defense, he appealed to his own accomplishments to make his case. All the while, many in the crowd could be heard as they applauded his many accomplishments. Though none can know their hearts, the likelihood is that they were not exercising discernment while he spoke. Rather, they were quite happy to have their ears tickled for a bit and fell into the trap of spiritual gullibility: Applaud those who claim to have done great things for the Lord.

---

[6] Rick Warren, "Rick Warren Address SBC Messengers in Anaheim (2022)" (https://www.youtube.com/watch?v=MBsT1zFmC3E).

Hearing and reading Warren's statements immediately brings to mind the story of Nebuchadnezzar's pride and punishment of Daniel 4:30–32:

> Is not this great Babylon, which I have built by my mighty power as a royal residence and for the glory of my majesty?" While the words were still in the king's mouth, there fell a voice from heaven, "O King Nebuchadnezzar, to you it is spoken: The kingdom has departed from you, and you shall be driven from among men, and your dwelling shall be with the beasts of the field. And you shall be made to eat grass like an ox, and seven periods of time shall pass over you, until you know that the Most High rules the kingdom of men and gives it to whom he will."

Such boasting in oneself is never a good thing, but it is absolutely tragic when used to make what is supposed to be a theological defense. For Nebuchadnezzar, the judgment of God was that he be turned into a madman. One may be excused if they think, looking at Warren and the many like him, that they have already been turned to madmen by the Lord.

Of course, Warren could not offer a biblical defense or theological argument for why women should be permitted to preach and pastor because there is none to be made. As if to prove this, he then followed up his self-boasting with a question: "Are we to keep bickering over secondary issues? Or are we going to keep the main thing the main thing? This will make God smile."

Concluding his argument, Warren argued that the issue of women in church leadership is really just a *secondary* issue. So, why bicker over it? It's secondary. Move along.

But it is not a secondary issue. It is primary. And to say otherwise is tantamount to totally rejecting God's Word.

Thankfully, many in the Southern Baptist Convention knew Warren and Saddleback were in serious error. The SBC made the biblical choice to disfellowship Saddleback and Warren.[7]

---

[7] Ben Zeisloft, "Rick Warren's Church Overwhelmingly Disfellowshipped from SBC," *The Sentinel*, June 14, 2023, https://republicsentinel.com/articles/rick-warrens-church-overwhelmingly-disfellowshipped-from-sbc.

Men Reclaiming the Pulpit

We could continue looking at other leaders like Warren or examine how even the Roman Catholic church is experiencing pressure to begin ordaining women as priests, but hopefully the reader will understand at this point that this is a serious issue in our day.

The pulpit has been encircled by feminists, and effeminate men are ready to hand it over. Egalitarians have only sinking sand to stand upon, but they continue to stand because far too few are willing to push back against them. But, with just one push, their entire kingdom would crumble. So, let us push back against their agenda and simply say once more that Sally cannot preach because she has not been called or equipped to do so. Men need to stand up and reclaim the pulpit.

Now, of course, such speech will upset a lot of people. Over the past few decades, the concerted effort of the feminist agenda has been to demonstrate the adage, "Anything men can do, women can do better. And, in fact, women are so much better at doing those things, and so far superior, that men really aren't needed at all." So, to make the claim that women *cannot* preach is rattling to many. The objections to such claims are nearly endless. These objections also employ little to no Bible or simply twist what the Scriptures say.

Christians need to recognize the truth that, historically and traditionally speaking, one would have been hard pressed to find a respectable denomination ordaining women before the mid-twentieth century. Then, seemingly in correspondence with the rise of feminist teachings and philosophies, many formerly respectable denominations threw away the principles of Scripture, adopted a posture of Satanic egalitarianism, questioned the validity and authority of Scripture, and ordained women to preach. "Did God really say..." quickly gave way to, "God did not say, or, if He did say, we know better than Him, anyway."

Before the twentieth century, just as there were few women being sent off to war, there were few women being ordained for ministry. There were, of course, exceptions to this, though. For example, the United Church of Christ had Antoinette Brown, who was ordained in the 1850s. At the time, the UCC did not recognize her ordination, but the seeds had been planted. Is it any surprise that they are one of the most backslidden denominations in the world today?

While the argument rages on within the Presbyterian Church of America, the Presbyterian Church of the United States of America decided decades ago to throw the Bible out the window of their fast-moving car in favor of actively doing whatever perversities their sinful hearts desired. By the end of the twentieth century, the PCUSA wasn't just ordaining women; they were flying the rainbow flag to support homosexuals. By 2022, they are numbered amongst those denominations that actively invite drag queens to come and share with adults and children within their "churches." Clearly, endorsing women as "preachers" and "pastors" makes for a quick downward spiral in denominations and their churches.

The Quakers also have a history of women in leadership. Though they do not ordain ministers, opting instead to permit multiple members from their congregations to teach and preach as they feel compelled, they have permitted and encouraged many women into the role of leadership. Those churches that follow in their theological footsteps, unsurprisingly, care little for the need of God's calling upon a minister of the gospel and seem to be willing to ordain anything that moves and breathes.

The list could go on, but the point is this: every church that permits, allows, or encourages the ordination of women into pastoral leadership, or allows them into the pulpit to preach, is on a downward spiral into theological liberalism. There is no alternative. Once God's created order is denied, the entire book of Genesis is ignored. When the first book of the Bible is ignored and denied, the other 65 books of the Bible quickly follow suit. After all, a house can hardly stand without a foundation, and Genesis is the foundation of the Bible. Remove it, and the house crumbles.

The upholding of God's created order through gender roles is essential to remaining faithful to Scripture. Get rid of gender roles, and in a few years' time, drag queens will be taking over the pulpits. Ignore the created order and gender roles and transsexual lesbians with preferred pronouns like "they/them" or "zis/zey" take to the pulpits to preach about tearing down patriarchal structures in the name of mother god.

Some may accuse me at this point of committing the slippery slope fallacy. Some may even say that I'm scaremongering; that there is no evidence that there is a direct correlation between the ordination of women and the theological drift and subsequent destruction of a denomination. But such an argument ignores the examples I listed above and denies the biblical witness. If Scripture itself states that women can't preach or pastor, then nothing else matters in the argument. They simply can't preach or pastor.

A church cannot remain conservative and ordain women to ministry. Once a church or denomination permits women into its leadership ranks, it has already turned theologically liberal. It is not just beginning to drift; it turned long ago. It can still call itself theologically conservative and employ similar language to what it did in the past, but it's all just empty gesturing. A spade is a spade even if it calls itself a club.

The voter identifying as a conservative but voting for a woman's right to choose an abortion is a liberal, no matter which way they spin it. The person calling themselves a conservative and orthodox Christian but encouraging and permitting the ordination of women is a theologically liberal heretic, no matter which way they spin it. Words matter and the definitions of words matter. A Christian cannot be conservative, orthodox, or faithful to God and His

Word if they in any way support the ordination of women into leadership roles.

The moment women take the pulpit, a church's fate is sealed. Unless it repents and turns from its wickedness, the downward spiral will bring it ever deeper into the embrace of Satan and further from the bosom of the Father. The only slippery part of this slope is how fast a church can wind its way down the spiral of sin. The question is not, "*Will* such a church self-destruct after adopting such a posture?" but, "*When* will such a church self-destruct after adopting such a posture?"

4

Fencing the Pulpit

In most Reformed churches, there is an understanding that the Lord's Supper and the Communion Table are to be protected from outsiders. Or perhaps a better way of wording it is this: outsiders need to be protected from the Lord's Table. This is because the Apostle Paul warns in 1 Corinthians 11:27–32:

> Whoever, therefore, eats the bread or drinks the cup of the Lord in an unworthy manner will be guilty concerning the body and blood of the Lord. Let a person examine himself, then, and so eat of the bread and drink of the cup. For anyone who eats and drinks without discerning the body eats and drinks judgment on himself. That is why many of you are weak and ill, and some have died. But if we judged ourselves truly, we would not be judged. But when we are judged by the Lord, we are disciplined so that we may not be condemned along with the world.

Outsiders must not be permitted participation in the Lord's Supper because the one who partakes unworthily actually eats and drinks judgment upon themselves. It would be unloving for us to permit those who are lost and unsaved from participating in our most joyous feast because the judgment against them would be severe.

We refer to this work as "barring" or "fencing" the Lord's Table. Typically, in order to make certain that those who are participating are saved members in good standing of their churches, and not under church discipline, we insist that only those members of the church who are in good standing may be permitted to partake. It is a good work for churches to do, and I implore all those reading to follow suit.

For similar reasons, it is essential that Christians learn to fence, or bar, the pulpit. Stepping behind the sacred desk may not be taken as seriously as it once was, but that does not make it any less serious—or dangerous. This is extraordinarily important business that we are about, and the one who enters a pulpit to break the bread of God's Word must be biblically qualified. The one who is unqualified will not be filled with God's Holy Spirit in a way that is conducive to preaching the Word of God. Without the help of God, the unqualified will not preach God's Word, but will instead do violence to it.

Let the reader understand: If Sally takes to the pulpit, violence will be done to God's Word.

So, knowing this, why have so many permitted Sally to take to the pulpit anyway? B. B. Warfield offers some powerful historical insight.

The Apostle Paul and B. B. Warfield vs. Radical Feminism

The first quarter of the twenty-first century has unequivocally proven that radical feminism is destructive to the family, church, and society. Feminism has assaulted education, attempting to teach children that subverted gender roles are the norm rather than an oddity. It has attacked the work force so that, today, most women are unable to not work. It has even led to the legalization of the murder of the unborn in the abortion movement. At its core, it is antithetical to Scripture and a Christian worldview. Because feminism views the world through an individualistic lens, rather than a familial and communal lens, it is incapable of adopting Scripture's teaching on the role of men and women in the family, church, and society.[1]

Over a century ago, the great Princeton theologian B.B. Warfield saw the feminist movement for what it was—anti-Christian—and wrote with an almost prophetic voice:

> The difference in conclusions between Paul and the feminist movement of today is rooted in a fundamental difference in their points of view relative to the constitution of the human race. To Paul, the human race is made up of families, and every several organism—the church included—is composed of families, united together by this or that bond. The relation of the sexes in the family follow it therefore into the church. To the feminist movement the human race is made up of individuals; a woman is just another individual by the side of the man, and it can see no reason for any differences in dealing with the two.

---

[1] See David J. Ayer, "The Inevitability of Failure: The Assumptions and Implementations of Modern Feminism," in *Recovering Biblical Manhood and Womanhood: A Response to Evangelical Feminism*, eds. John Piper and Wayne Grudem (Wheaton, IL: Crossway, 2012), 389.

> And, indeed, if we can ignore the great fundamental natural difference of sex and destroy the great fundamental social unit of the family in the interest of individualism, there does not seem any reason why we should not wipe out the differences established by Paul between the sexes in the church — except, of course, the authority of Paul.[2]

If the pulpit will be fenced and preaching made great again, these cultural and historical considerations need to be dealt with.

Feminism Leading the Charge in Rejecting Paul's Teaching

B. B. Warfield received his anthropological and theological views from the Bible. Since the Bible speaks about the importance of distinct gender roles, and since it clearly defies the very idea of expressive individualism, Warfield combatted the feminism of his day. Perhaps he knew what would happen if it was

---

[2] B. B. Warfield, "Paul on Women Speaking in Church" (https://www.pcahistory.org/documents/paulonwomenspeaking.html).

allowed to run rampant without opposition: Women doing violence to God's Word from pulpits. He, of course, would have had no trouble fencing the pulpit from those unworthy and incapable of preaching God's Word.

Many would call Warfield's comments sexist, and that's hardly shocking considering where his teaching came from: Christ Himself. After all, if the world hated Jesus first, should it not also hate us, His followers? The Apostles, who preached the teachings of Jesus far and wide, knew this firsthand.

The Apostle Paul's comments in Scripture are likely the most widely known in this regard. He is often called misogynistic by today's society, which has been, in large part, dominated by feminist philosophy and rhetoric over the past century. It is almost unimaginable that any man would have the audacity to write what Paul, or Warfield, did. In 1 Timothy 2:12, Paul writes that he does not permit women to speak in church. First Timothy 3:1–13 and Titus 1:5–9 make the case that only men are permitted to the position of elder or overseer. Ephesians 5:22–24 calls for women to submit to their husbands and for husbands to be head of the household. Time and again, Paul's teaching is that men are to lead their wives and families in the love of Christ and wives are to submit to their husband's rule.

As we have seen, Scripture teaches that there is a difference between the sexes, instituted in God's creation of male and female at the beginning (1 Tim. 2:13), and those differences are to be honored and realized to their fullest potential within the confines of relationships. It is not the individualistic but the familial attitude that allows for the flourishing of both sexes.

The Family as the Solution

Even as we speak of fencing the pulpit, it is obvious that many will consider such a position and attitude unloving and judgmental, perhaps even hateful. The trouble lies in the idea that man, or woman, can be an island to him or herself. Once individualism runs rampant and the view that the family is vitally important is done away with, the design, intent, and teleology of Creation is virtually inverted on itself. Though not the only culprit, the turning of the family upside down has had negative implications upon the church. If a woman believes her worth, value, and dignity are found in a position outside the home, and if she views standing behind the pulpit as giving the greatest worth and value, then obviously she will seek to stand behind the pulpit. If she believes the lies of feminism that a woman who submits to her husband at home is worthless, but a woman who submits to her boss at work is valuable, then of course she will seek to leave the family.

Having left the family and unshackled herself from the authority of her husband, the next step is to leave behind the authority of God's Word. Rather than raise children (which can be painful even after giving birth), the woman entrapped by feminism would rather seek a vocation outside the home, where she believes she can rule over men. If she believes, "Anything a man can do, I can do better," she will eye those roles and positions that have been distinctly reserved for men in order to prove her point. The fenced pulpit will be one of the highest places she seeks to infiltrate. This is, in part, what God meant when He told Eve, "I will surely multiply your pain in childbearing; in pain you shall bring forth children. Your desire shall be contrary to your husband, but he shall rule over you" (Gen. 3:16).

The solution, then, is found within a robust anthropology that seeks to be faithful to the truth of the

Word of God. If Sally is going to learn that she cannot preach, then the family *is* the solution. A woman must learn that there is no substitute for a wife and mother at home, caring for her family. In fact, it is plain that her greatest worth and value is found there.

Churches must, like Warfield, promote an understanding of the sexes that encapsulates the conservative, complementarian view of gender roles, especially relating to their roles within the family and household. Men and women are equal in personhood, worth, and value. However, men and women are created for different purposes that the other is not meant to fulfill. This is true for the household as it is elsewhere, and when men and women are viewed in light of communion with Christ and with the knowledge that "it is not good for the man to be alone" (Gen. 2:18), a familial, rather than an individualistic, concept of humanity will be embraced. A rejection of a familial perspective of the sexes in favor of an individualistic view will promote contrary worldviews like radical feminism.

Ephesians 5:22–6:4 makes it abundantly clear that there is to be a structure within the home, which corresponds to the structure of the church. At the head of the household stands man as the husband, father, and leader. He both provides for his family and protects his family, while also leading his wife and children in spiritual disciplines. Equal to him, yet under his authority and rule, stands his wife. The wife and mother of the home has much she is commanded to do and, indeed, much she can do, i.e., Proverbs 31 depicts a woman who not only cares for her household and nurtures the people in her home, but also tends to the finances of the home in various ways. However, she is continually to submit to the authority of her husband. Just like the Christian finds freedom in Christ to obey His commands, the Christian wife finds freedom to serve her household and lead her children in a plethora of ways.

Beneath the father and the mother are the children of the household. While neither parent should needlessly provoke their child to wrath, they are to train their children up, cultivating spiritual disciplines within them. This means, within the social hierarchy of the home, children are equal in worth, value, and dignity to their parents, but are underneath their rule and jurisdiction.

The radical feminist movement, on the other hand, would see this all done away with in favor of a household that sees all persons submitting to the rule of the woman who, in this vision, is actually not at home, anyway. This is because, in the feminist vision, woman supplants man as the leader, ruler, provider, and protector of the household. With the vision of the home disoriented, it is no surprise that the vision of the church and society go with it as well. No longer are men the sole governors of a local church, who act as under-shepherds with Christ as the true Over-Shepherd. Rather, in a dismissal of a text like 1 Timothy 3:2, women are put into positions of power they were never meant to hold. Thus, Christ is dishonored as typology is totally ignored and women possess the power that men were to wield to point others to Jesus.

Society follows suit, as women enter positions of power that, though they are perhaps capable of functioning within, were not intended for them. (Pastoring and preaching, of course, are positions she is incapable of functioning within. She has no ability in this area because God has not granted it.) Women end up carrying burdens they were never meant to bear, and society is the worse for wear. This is fundamentally because they have rejected the authority of God's Word. Returning to Warfield, he would go on to write:

> It all, in the end, comes back to the authority of the apostles, as founders of the church. We may like what Paul says, or we may not like it. We may be willing to do what he commands, or we may not be willing to do it. But there is no room for doubt of what he says. And he certainly would say to us what he said to the Corinthians: "What? Was it from you that the word of God went forth? Or came it to you alone?" Is this Christianity ours — to do with as we like? Or is it God's religion, receiving its laws from him through the apostles?

As Warfield noted, the issue is not so much whether one likes what Scripture has to say, or whether one even agrees with what Scripture says. It does not matter, honestly, if someone thinks it "mean" to fence the pulpit. These things must still be done.

The point is, God has prescribed laws within His Word for both individuals and families. When Christians possess a robust theology of anthropology, they will recognize that God's laws for men and women are designed with the good intention of causing the greatest of human flourishing. The goal of creation, after all, is not a desert island, but a garden city wherein the people of God, saved by Christ, dwell *together* with their King forever. This is a Kingdom comprised of a family, rather than merely expressive individuals.

Thus, a familial lens, which honors Christ as Lord, is essential for a proper understanding of the sexes and true human flourishing of both men and women. A familial lens is essential if Sally, and all her supporters, will ever learn that she simply cannot preach. Those who desire the flourishing of families, churches, and societies must fence the pulpit; there is, quite simply, no other way. Only those who are biblically qualified may take part in this great work.

5

The Battle Won by Truth

Jesus promised in John 8:31–32, "If you abide in my word, you are truly my disciples, and you will know the truth, and the truth will set you free." The truth is a raging fire that will burn down the strongholds of the enemy, set the captives free, and conquer the liars and their lies.

We know the truth of the Word of God is our main weapon in this battle and we know the truth will ultimately prevail. But are there any steps that we can take to fight this battle well with the truth we know from Scripture? Yes, of course there are.

I suggest employing the following tactics:

These truths need to be taught to our sons and daughters while they're still young.

It is essential for pastors to preach the full counsel of God's Word. Sunday School coloring page hours, children's church babysitting clubs, and Wednesday night pizza hang outs simply won't cut it anymore. They never did.

We live in an age that is decidedly antagonistic towards the things of God, and we can't have our kids grow up by coloring pictures of Jonah and the big fish and expect them to have any understanding of God's design for the sexes, much less be equipped to give a robust defense of biblical anthropology. If we want our children to understand the necessity and goodness of gender roles, especially as it pertains to the pulpit, then they must be faithfully taught biblical doctrine from God's Word. If Harry and Sally are going to come to terms with the fact that Sally can't preach while living in a culture that says Sally can do anything, then the man in the pulpit must be unwaveringly strong in his convictions and passionate in his declarations of God's Word. Cowards need not apply. This is a time for bold men of courage.

It is a mistake, however, to think this is only the pastor's responsibility. Shepherding most often happens at home. That's where our children are most often formatively shaped. Frederick Douglas is purported to have said that "It is easier to build strong children, than to repair broken men." Just as neglecting to preach clearly and faithfully on gender roles will only produce broken and weak men and women who do not understand what their God-intended roles actually are, weak parenting will accomplish much the same. Parents must be strong and rise to the occasion, faithfully modeling the biblical gender roles for our children. So, fathers: Lead well. Mothers: Submit well.

Rather than fixing what is broken—which can take a lifetime—we must put in the hard work of teaching our children the goodness of gender roles while they're still children.

We must seek faithful church bodies to join with our families.

Imagine with me, if you would, a bleak and dystopian future where, due to some cataclysmic event, the world's oxygen has been poisoned. Now, everyone walks around in special suits that are designed to endure the catastrophic conditions.

But, once a week, these suits need an oxygen refill. Once a week, everyone must make their way to a refill station. Life literally depends on it.

Now, there's a place that is far from your home that has really good oxygen. You're more than welcome to it, though, and if you go to that refill station, it's guaranteed to get you through the week, strengthen you, and keep you going. But it's far.

Yet, there's a place right in your town—within walking distance even. But the oxygen they serve is weak; it's been polluted and is no longer pure. It might get you through the week, but it might not. Either way, it won't do a very good job of it, even if it does last you until the next refill. Your lungs will be weakened, and your strength will fail.

What would you choose? Most would say they'd travel to get the better oxygen. Only makes sense, right?

Yet, when it comes to hearing the Word of God rightly preached and proclaimed, how few are willing to travel! Yes, the Word is far more important to your spiritual health than even oxygen is to the physical body. You need the Word more than you need all else.

But, for the sake of ease and convenience, Christians will endure unsound teaching that has been corrupted by the things of this world. Some are willing to sit beneath unqualified men *and women* if it means they have convenience. They know the teaching they receive at these churches will not truly nourish or sustain them. In fact, it may fail them all together, as the spiritual life simply cannot survive off the spiritual equivalent of cotton candy and soda. Like the one in our story who settles for weaker oxygen, they settle for weak teaching and sinful "leaders" for the convenience of it.

Many excuses are made for why one cannot possibly hope to travel to find a sound church. But your spiritual life depends on it. You cannot effectively serve God apart from a steady diet of the unadulterated Word preached and proclaimed and the faithful gathering of the saints. Like the oxygen tank being refilled in our imagined scenario, the spirit must be fed weekly by God's Word rightly preached within a local church, surrounded by the saints of God.

Find a solid church to attend where God's Word is faithfully preached, the sacraments are administered, and worship is performed in Spirit and in Truth. If you must drive an hour to get there, it will be worth it. You might wonder how you will afford the gas, but you quite simply cannot afford not to go. The very life of your soul, and that of your family members, depends on it.

We must be bold enough to hold our leaders accountable to Scripture and be willing to leave an unfaithful and backslidden church.

Revelation 21:8 states, "But as for the cowardly, the faithless, the detestable, as for murderers, the sexually immoral, sorcerers, idolaters, and all liars, their portion will be in the lake that burns with fire and sulfur, which is the second death."

Cowardly Christians are an unacceptable oxymoron; a paradoxical impossibility. A Christian can no more be a coward than a moose can fly, or a plant speak. While a Christian may certainly feel fear for a time, they must eventually shun that fear in exchange for the courage that comes from knowing Christ and being known by Him.

We must be bold enough to believe the Scriptures and proclaim them. The world will likely hate you if you proclaim what I'm suggesting you must proclaim in this little book. Proclaim it anyway. Don't be cowardly. Press on, Christian solider.

We must be bold enough to hold our church leaders accountable. Church leaders must be bold enough to hold themselves and their congregations accountable. The point is that, when it comes to upholding orthodox doctrine, cowardliness cannot be permitted or rewarded. True doctrine must be upheld by faithful and bold saints.

We must be bold enough to leave sinful and backslidden churches. Now, no church is perfect. Every church is constantly reforming. And, while some churches do have serious problems, there are some who are genuinely called to the ministry of church "restoration" and "reformation." But, for the majority who read this work, it is likely unhealthy for you and your family to remain within a backslidden church.

So, let's make this vital distinction. If your "church" has a woman as a "pastor," then you need to get out. It's not a church, but a social gathering, and it is not worth your time. Do not delay. Get out and find a biblical church to attend.

On the other hand, if your church still has male leadership but he has adopted an egalitarian posture toward women in the pulpit, then it may still be necessary to leave immediately.

This is an unpopular truth: It is often a bad idea to stay in a backslidden church. If the church you attend has compromised on the area of gender roles, then it is likely time to leave that church. There are, occasionally, exceptions to this, but those exceptions merely prove the rule.

This is because a backslidden church will hardly ever experience reformation. If it does, it will take years. The question then becomes this: Do you have that time to invest in reformation, and does your family? If you have children, I suggest that you do not have the time necessary to see reformation occur. The years of their childhood are incredibly formative and vitally important in making certain they learn to love the church and God's Word. But a church that has compromised on gender roles will quickly compromise on many other things. Children in these settings often do not learn God's Word because the full counsel of His Word is not being preached. Furthermore, they do not learn to love the church because, typically, the "church" is a "church" in name only. Without the proper preaching of God's Word and faithful obedience to His standards for governing a church, spiritual growth is nigh an impossibility.

I understand the difficulty of what I write here. Some reading this, very likely, will not want to leave the church they are at. They might even feel compelled to dismiss this warning all together. But this is not something I speak of lightly. I truly believe, for the majority reading this, if you find yourself in an unbiblical church that has compromised in this area, you need to leave. Even if you're the pastor—a backslidden church will hardly recover. God can, of course, bring revival and reformation, but God has only allotted us so much time on this earth. The question you must ask is whether you are able to effectively serve the Lord where you are (and some truly are called to restoration-type ministries), or if you simply need to get out of dodge.

The true need of the day, in each of these scenarios, is courage. Even if your church does not currently wrestle with these issues, you must be bold to proclaim and live of the truth of Scripture as it pertains to God's design for the sexes.

Christians are to be bold in Christ and steadfast in their triumphant faith in the gospel. Let us go forth and sound the trumpets, march the battle lines, and shout glorious praise to our King of kings today! He is worthy to be praised, and half-hearted, frightened praise is intolerable. Mumbled or, worse yet, lip-synced praise, is insufferable. Lift the limp hand, strengthen the feeble knee, and lift your voice in song of praise and glorious truth today!

We must continue to preach and proclaim these truths even to those who disagree.

Those who have grown up and have been influenced by the world must be taught the whole counsel of Scripture too, and especially about God's order for men and women. Some of them will respond antagonistically to this doctrine. They're not a lost cause. I wouldn't have written half this booklet if I thought they were. Rather, we must pray to God, entrusting them to the care of a sovereign King who raises the spiritually dead and changes hearts. We must trust that, through the faithful preaching of God's Word, God can bring not only salvation, but even heart and worldview change to these individuals. It may seem impossible to us, but with God it is possible that they will even learn to love God's design in gender roles.

A few years back, a young married couple visited the church I was pastoring. Both had grown up in church, but neither had a strong grasp on doctrines such as the role of men and women. In a story that can perhaps be repeated in many households, the husband had grown up in a matriarchal home. The mother ruled, especially when it came to spiritual matters. His mother prayed, read the Bible, and led devotions. His father was present for this but acquiesced his leadership to his wife. This young man simply thought this was the norm.

The young man's wife grew up in denominations that have long permitted the ordination of women into leadership. She had even sat under women "pastors." She simply grew up believing it was a job for both men and women and never questioned her experiences. She thought it was commonplace throughout church history for women to serve in leadership roles and capacities.

By the providence of God, on one of those first Sundays they were visiting, it just so happened the text I was preaching through brought up the roles of men and women. I, without knowing their background, simply preached the text of Ephesians 5. I preached God's design for the household. Then, a few weeks later, preaching another text, I cross-referenced 1 Timothy 3 to describe what an elder was: a biblically qualified and faithful man. I even explained with Scripture how women simply could not enter the role of elder.

It wouldn't be until months later that this couple would sit down with me and tell me their story. Then, at the end of our conversation, they thanked me for being faithful and showing them the truth of God's Word. They recognized what they had grown up with was wrong and they would now strive towards operating within God's parameters for the sexes as outlined in His Word.

I share that story not to toot my own horn or inflame my ego. Rather, I share that because I've heard other pastors share similar stories and have had other people come to me with similar claims. This is not unusual when a pastor is faithful to preach God's Word. As Martin Luther once said, "I did nothing; the Word did everything."

So, pastors: preach the Word!

Christians: encourage your pastors to preach the Word, pray for them to preach the Word, and thank them when they preach the Word! Most of all, praise the Lord for faithful, Holy Spirit-filled, and biblically qualified men who preach and teach the Word with boldness and courage!

The Christian who earnestly desires biblical fidelity must hold fast to the Word of God even when it is unpopular. When encountering those who insist that women ought to be ordained into ministry, it is essential to stand upon God's Word and do righteous battle for the truth by the truth. As Peter called upon us to sanctify Jesus as the Lord of our hearts and lives, and to always be ready to give an account of our beliefs in 1 Peter 3:15, so too must we be able to defend the truth. Retreat is not an option. Silence in this matter amounts to cowardice. Sally cannot preach. Christ said so. And, if Christ is Lord at all, He must be Lord of all.

The duty of every follower of Christ is to recognize His Lordship over the entirety of His creation. We must uphold His Word and acknowledge that, in His Word, the Lord has created a distinction between the sexes. This is a vital, good, and beautiful doctrine to uphold that will promote great flourishing within our churches, homes, and society.

May the Lord graciously grant His servants courage to proclaim the truth and may He send us revival and reformation through the faithful preaching of His Word.

Made in the USA
Middletown, DE
22 November 2025